Polish Cooking

Contents

*P*olish cuisine is not a single, unchanging notion.

The first Polish cookbook was written in 1682 (before King Sobieski's Vienna campaign!) In its introduction, the author, Stanisław Czerniecki, defended himself: "one should not feel offended that my first book begins with Polish dishes...". Western ways of cooking were already familiar to the Polish nobles' kitchens. For centuries Polish cuisine had absorbed and adapted French, Italian, Lithuanian and Jewish dishes. Oriental spices were not alien to it; some foreign vegetables and fruits brought by Queen Bona to Poland were widely accepted, competing with the native favorites – cabbage, apples and pears.

Polish cuisine still thrives and grows, as it is simply everything Poles eat – in their home country and wherever they live around the world. Polish cuisine is an indispensable element of Polish culture and a marker of cultural and social development. It is spoken of mainly during traditional holidays and the meals associated with them, but every heart cherishes some favorite Polish dishes prepared by grandmother or mother for everyday meals. We come back to them eagerly, whether it be roll-ups, ryemeal soup, sauerkraut stew or crepes with farmer cheese and cherry preserves, because in this way we return to the family home of our childhood. We hope that you will find such recipes in this book, that you will refresh your memories of them and will pass their tradition to the next generation.

Herring in oil

Rinse herring (if very salty soak in cold water for an hour), slice into bite-size pieces or strips, place in a jar and cover with oil. Add spices. After 2–3 days the herring is perfect. It can be kept in the fridge for about 2 weeks (remember: the herring should remain covered with oil). Serve with finely chopped onion or onion slices, garnished with lemon, parsley or dill.

Herring (rollmops)

Soak herring in water for 24 hours (change water several times). Cut off heads and remove gut, keep milt. Prepare fillets, remove bones, then spread each fillet with mustard, sprinkle with pepper and garnish with half the onion (chopped). Roll up chopped onion and pickles in each fillet, fasten with a toothpick and place in a jar. Boil vinegar with spices, the rest of the onion and water (proportion: 1 c. water to $^1/_2$ c. vinegar), then allow to cool. Remove sac from milt, rub milt through a sieve, mix with oil and combine with cooled vinegar marinade. Fill the jar of rolled herring with marinade, leave in the fridge for 2–3 days. Can be kept for 10 days in a cool place. Serve as anappetizer, or as a main course with baked potatoes.

Ingredients:

Herring in oil:
- *8 salt herring fillets*
- *1 onion*
- *$^1/_2$ c. olive or sunflower oil*
- *2–3 allspice seeds*
- *2–3 peppercorns*
- *1 bay leaf*

Herring (rollmops):
- *4 whole salt herrings*
- *2 pickles*
- *1 large onion*
- *1–2 T. prepared mustard*
- *wine vinegar (6%)*
- *bay leaf*
- *ground pepper*
- *sugar*
- *2–3 T. olive or sunflower oil*

Carp in aspic

Scale and rinse carp. Remove gut, but do not rinse inside. Fillet and salt. Leave for about half an hour. Slice onion, clean and wash vegetables, carp head and edible organs (liver, milt). Put in a pot and add cold water (approx.3 pt.). Add spices and bring to a boil. Place carp fillets in boiling bouillon and simmer 10-20 minutes on a law flame. If fish is served on Christmas Eve, place it on a deep platter, restoring its original shape (including head). Strain fish stock (boil off if more than 1 pt.), add salt and pepper to taste. Soak gelatin in a small quantity of fish stock, add to the rest and mix. Garnish with carrot (covering fish eye), cover with fish stock and leave in a cool place until set. Fillets may be served without the head, covered with aspic and canned peas. On Christmas Eve, carp is served with prepared horseradish and white bread (preferably challah).

Ingredients:

- *2¹/₂ – 3 lb. carp*
- *3 large onions*
- *2 carrots*
- *2 parsnips*
- *a few allspice seeds and peppercorns*
- *2 bay leaves*
- *1 t. plain gelatin*
- *salt*
- *ground pepper*

7

Jellied calf's or pig's feet

Rinse feet and split bones, rinse meat.
Clean, wash and cut vegetables
and onion into large pieces.
Add bay leaves, allspice, peppercorns
and garlic (best tied up in cheesecloth).
Add slightly salted water and simmer
on very low flame for 2 hours,
until meat falls off the bones.
Take meat out, cut into small pieces,
strain bouillon, cover meat with bouillon,
add salt and pepper to taste.
Add sliced carrots or arrange them
in a jelling form previously rinsed with cold
water. Pour liquid and meat into the form
and leave it to cool. Before serving,
scrape off congealed fat
and turn jelly onto a serving platter.

Ingredients:

- *2 lb. calf's or pig's feet*
- *³/₄ lb. boneless lean pork or veal*
- *½ lb. soup vegetables (carrot, parsnip, leek and celery root)*
- *1 large onion*
- *1–2 bay leaves*
- *1–2 garlic cloves*
- *a few allspice seeds and peppercorns*
- *salt*
- *ground pepper*

Steak tartare

Remove sinew and rinse beef tenderloin. Grind, add mustard, olive oil, 1 egg yolk, parsley, salt and pepper to taste. Form it into flattened mounds on a plate, place fresh egg yolk on top of each mound. Surround mounds with finely chopped onion, finely diced pickles and capers. Serve immediately.

Ingredients:

- $3/4 - 1$ lb. beef tenderloin
- 2 egg yolks
- 1 large onion
- 1 T. prepared mustard
- 1 T. olive oil
- 2 small pickles
- 3 T. capers
- 1 t. finely chopped parsley
- salt
- ground pepper to taste

Cooked vegetable salad

Cook vegetables in a large quantity of salted water (you may also use soup vegetables from making bouillon). Drain and peel boiled potatoes. Dice vegetables and pickles. Add canned green peas, onion, pickled mushrooms, and peeled chopped apple sprinkled with lemon juice. Add mayonnaise and gently mix (best to use two forks). Add salt, pepper and sugar to taste. Serve on lettuce leaves, garnish with tomato wedges.

Ingredients:

- $1/2$ lb. potatoes (boiled with skin)
- $1/4$ lb. carrots
- $1/4$ lb. celery
- $1/8$ lb. parsnip
- 1 can green peas
- $1/4$ lb. pickles
- 1 large apple (not sweet)
- 1 t. finely chopped onion
- 1 t. lemon juice
- 1 T. finely chopped pickled mushrooms (optional)
- 1 c. mayonnaise
- salt
- ground pepper
- sugar

Garnish:
- lettuce
- tomato

Tripe

*T*horoughly wash tripe, scald with boiling water, scrub, cut off dark ends, rinse once again, put into boiling water and cook covered for 15 minutes. Drain, put into freshy salted boiling water, cover and cook on a low flame until completely tender (about 4 hours). Drain, save some stock, cool and cut into thin strips. Clean, wash and finely chop carrot, celery and parsnip. Peel all but one onion, slice finely, add to the vegetables, then add boiling bouillon, add tripe and 1 T. butter, cook about 45 minutes covered. Finely chop the remaining onion, fry in 1 T. butter until transparent but not browned, add flour mix with 2 T. water, bring to a boil, adding a little tripe stock. Add to tripe, bring to a boil, add salt, pepper and red pepper to taste if desire. Serve with grated yellow cheese and fresh rolls.

Ingredients:

- *2 lb. beef tripe*
- *2 c. rich beef bouillon*
- *2 lb. vegetables (carrot, celery root, parsnip, leek)*
- *³/₄ lb. onion*
- *2 T. butter*
- *1 T. flour*
- *salt*
- *nutmeg*
- *ground pepper*
- *hot red pepper*
- *ginger*
- *marjoram*
- *bay leaf*
- *allspice*
- *2 T. grated yellow cheese*

Bean soup à la Brètonne

*R*inse dry beans and soak overnight in cold water. Cook in the same water, slightly salted, together with bacon, until beans are tender. Peel onion, dice, brown slightly in cooking oil, add flour, make a roux, add some bean stock and tomato paste. Mix and add to beans. Dice Vienna sausage (without wrappers) and bacon, add to bean soup and bring it to a boil. Add salt, a pinch of paprika, and sugar to taste if desired.

Ingredients:

- $^3/_4$ *lb. dry white beans (preferably lima beans)*
- $^1/_4$ *lb. slab bacon*
- $^1/_4$ *lb. Vienna sausage*
- *2 T. cooking oil*
- *1 medium onion*
- *5–6 T. tomato paste*
- *1 T. flour*
- *salt*
- *sugar*
- *paprika*

Bigos
(meat & sauerkraut stew)

*F*inely chop sauerkraut, scald with a small quantity of boiling water and cook together with rinsed mushrooms about 1 hour. Rinse, salt and fry meat together with diced fatback. Add to sauerkraut together with slab bacon, add wine and cook for another 40 minutes until tender. Take out meat, slab bacon and mushrooms and dice them. Remove sausage skin, slice sausage and add to the stew. Gently brown onion until transparent, add flour, mix with 1 T. water and add to the stew. Bring the stew to a boil. Add salt, pepper and sugar to taste.

Note: You may add different kinds of meat to the stew (leftover roast meat, game or poultry). *Bigos* is very tasty when reheated.

Ingredients:

- *2–2 1/2 lb. sauerkraut*
- *1/2 lb. boneless pork*
- *1/2 lb. veal*
- *1/2 lb. sausage*
- *1/4 lb. slab bacon*
- *1/4 oz. dry mushrooms*
- *2 oz. fatback*
- *1 large onion*
- *1/2 c. red wine (optional)*
- *1 T. flour*
- *salt*
- *ground pepper*
- *sugar*

Beet sour

*P*eel, rinse and slice beets and cover with pre-boiled lukewarm water in a crockery bowl or a jar. Add a slice of rye bread with the crust, cover the mouth of the jar or bowl with cheesecloth and let stand at room temperature for a few days. Then strain through cheesecloth, pour into a bottle and seal it. Store in a cool place (in the basement or fridge).

Ingredients:

- *3–3 1/2 lb. beets*
- *slice of rye bread with the crust*

Traditional Christmas Eve barszcz with mushroom-filled uszka (pierogi for soup)

Ingredients:

- *1 lb. beet*
- *½ lb. soup vegetables (carrot, parsnip, celery root, leek)*
- *2 t. butter*
- *salt*
- *ground pepper*
- *sugar*
- *garlic clove*
- *1–2 c. beet sour*
- *mushroom stock*
- *1 T. finely chopped parsley*

Clean, wash and cut vegetables. Peel, rinse and slice beets. Add cold salted water (approx. 6 c.). Simmer with 1 t. butter until vegetables are tender. Strain. Add garlic crushed with salt, beet sour, a little mushroom stock (see *uszka* recipe next page), sugar and pepper to taste. Before serving add 1 t. butter to hot soup and sprinkle with finely chopped parsley. Serve hot with *uszka*.

Uszka

Soak rinsed mushrooms in cold water
overnight. Simmer until tender in enough water
to have a little mushroom stock to set aside.
Peel, finely chop and fry onion
in cooking oil until light golden.
Grind mushrooms, add bread crumbs,
onion, parsley, salt and pepper to taste.
Sift flour onto a breadboard, add egg,
salt and approx. 1 c. lukewarm water.
Knead dough until elastic. Divide into two
portions. Roll out one part thin.
Keep the second under a bowl so it does
not dry. Cut dough sheets into $1^1/_2$-inch squares,
put filling in the middle of each, fold in half
to form a triangle and pinch the edges together.

Ingredients:

Dough:

- $^3/_4$ *c. flour*
- *1 egg*
- *salt*

Filling:

- *1 $^1/_2$ c. dried mushrooms*
- *1 T. bread crumbs*
- *1 small onion*
- *1 T. finely chopped parsley*
- *1 t. cooking oil*
- *salt*
- *ground pepper*

Cold barszcz

*R*inse baby beets and their greens, cut into short strips. Peel and cut beet and cook together with baby beets in a small amount of water until tender, adding a pinch of sugar. Just before taking it off the flame, add citric acid or 1 t. lemon juice. Take out beet. Mix sour milk with cream, add cooled baby beets with beet stock, chopped dill, peeled and diced cucumber, stir and cool. Serve with quartered hard-boiled eggs. You may also add diced roast veal.

Ingredients:

- *8 c. sour unpasteurized milk*
- *a few T. thick sour cream*
- *1 bunch baby beets*
- *1 bunch dill*
- *dash of citric acid or 1 t. lemon juice*
- *1 medium beet*
- *1 cucumber*
- *2 hard-boiled eggs*
- *salt*
- *sugar*

Split pea soup with smoked meat

Rinse split peas and soak in cold water
overnight. Cook in the same water,
strain and rub through a sieve.
Cook soup vegetables and bacon in 7 c. salted
water to make a bouillon. Rub the cooked
vegetables through a sieve.
Add sieved peas and vegetables to the boullion.
Fry finely chopped onion until light golden,
add flour, make a roux, add a few T. cold
water to make a smooth mixture
and add it to the soup. Crush garlic with salt,
crush marjoram, add to the soup
and bring it to a boil. Serve hot soup
with diced bacon.
You may also add butter-fried
white bread croutons.

Ingredients:

- $^3/_4$ lb. split peas
- $^1/_2$ lb. soup vegetables (carrot, parsnip, celery root, leek)
- $^1/_4$ lb. slab bacon
- 1 onion
- 1 T. butter
- 1 rounded T. flour
- 1–2 garlic cloves
- marjoram
- salt

Sauerkraut soup

Clean and rinse vegetables. Put them in 7 c. cold salted water, add a bay leaf and bring to a boil.
Drain sauerkraut and set the sauerkraut juice aside. Finely chop sauerkraut, cover with boiling strained bouillon, add bacon and bring to a boil.
Fry finely chopped onion together with finely diced fatback until the onion is light golden.
Add separately browned flour, mix with a small quantity of water, add to the bouillon and bring to a boil. Take the bacon out, dice and put back in the soup. Add sauerkraut juice, and pepper and salt to taste.

Ingredients:

- $3/4$–1 lb. sauerkraut
- $1/4$ lb. slab bacon
- $1/2$ lb. soup vegetables (carrot, parsnip, celery root, leek)
- 2 oz. fatback
- 1 onion
- 3 T. flour
- salt
- ground pepper
- bay leaf

Barley soup

*R*inse barley groats, cover with cold water (2 c.), add 1 t. butter, simmer on low heat until tender (about 15 minutes). Soak mushrooms for a few hours and cook mushrooms, cleaned vegetables and giblets in 7 c. water. Strain the bouillon. Cut mushrooms and vegetables into strips. Cook peeled and diced potatoes in the bouillon. Combine the bouillon with the barley, mushrooms and vegetables, and salt to taste. Before serving, add 1 t. butter and parsley.

Ingredients:

- *1/2 lb. soup vegetables (carrot, parsnip, celery root, leek)*
- *chicken wings, neck and hearts*
- *2–3 dried mushrooms*
- *$\frac{1}{2}$ c. barley groats*
- *4–5 medium-sized potatoes*
- *2 t. butter*
- *1 t. chopped parsley*
- *salt*

Mushroom soup with square noodles (łazanki)

Cover well-rinsed mushrooms with cold water for 2 hours. Cook in the same water until tender, adding chopped onion. Clean and wash vegetables, cook in 7 c. salted water. Drain and combine the bouillon with drained mushroom stock. Brown the flour in cooking oil until it is a light-golden roux, add a few T. cold water. Add the roux to the bouillon with mushroom stock and bring to a boil. Add sour cream mixed with a small quantity of soup, add salt and pepper to taste and mushrooms cut into strips. Sprinkle with parsley. Serve with square noodles prepared in advance.

Square noodles: Sift flour onto a breadboard, break 1 egg on top of it, add salt and knead into dough, gradually adding lukewarm water. The resulting dough should be rather firm. Roll out thin and let dry. Sprinkle with flour, roll up into a wide roll. Cut the roll into $1/_2$-inch strips. Pile up a few strips and cut them into squares. Scatter over a floured board and let dry for a while. Drop into salted boiling water, stir, cook, drain, add 1 t. cooking oil.

Ingredients:

Soup:

- $^1/_2$ *lb. soup vegetables (carrot, parsnip, celery root, leek)*
- $1^1/_2$ *oz. dried mushrooms*
- *3 T. flour*
- *2 T. cooking oil*
- $^1/_2$ *c. sour cream*
- *1 t. finely chopped parsley*
- *salt*
- *pepper*

Łazanki:

- $^3/_4$ *c. flour*
- *1 egg*
- *salt*
- *1 t. cooking oil*

Ryemeal soup (żurek) with sausage

Cook a bouillon from soup vegetables and 6 c. water. Shortly before straining, add the sausage. Peel potatoes, cut into large cubes and cook in boiling, lightly salted bouillon. Mix flour with a few T. water, add to the bouillon along with ryemeal sour, sliced sausage, and garlic crushed with salt, and bring the soup to a boil.

Ingredients:

Ryemeal sour:

- *mix $^3/_4$ c. rye flour with 2 c. pre-boiled warm water. Pour into a jar or crockery bowl, cover with cheesecloth and let stand in a warm place for 4–5 days.*

Żurek:

- *$^1/_2$ lb. soup vegetables (carrot, parsnip, celery root, leek)*
- *$^1/_2$ lb. sausage*
- *1 lb. potatoes*
- *2 c. ryemeal sour*
- *1 rounded T. flour*
- *garlic clove*
- *salt*

Veal in paprika sauce with egg-batter dumplings

*R*inse the meat and pat dry, cut into small pieces, salt, sprinkle with pepper and part of the flour, then fry all sides in cooking oil briefly and place in a pot. Add butter, peeled and finely chopped onion and garlic crushed with salt, add $1/_2$ c. water and stew on a low flame for 40–45 minutes, adding more water as the sauce evaporates. When the meat is tender, add paprika, sprinkle and stir in the remaining flour and bring to a boil, then add sour cream. Serve with egg-batter dumplings.

Ingredients:

Veal in paprika sauce:

- *1–1$^1/_2$ lb. boneless veal (shoulder or neck)*
- *2 T. cooking oil*
- *2 T. flour*
- *1 t. butter*
- *1 large onion*
- *garlic clove*
- *$^1/_2$ c. sour cream*
- *salt*
- *ground pepper*
- *paprika*

Egg-batter dumplings:

- *1 c. flour*
- *1 egg*
- *salt*
- *1 t. butter (optional)*

Polish style veal brisket

Carefully rinse the veal brisket, pat dry, place flat on a cutting board and cut where the meat divides into two parts, then widen the "pocket" with your hand. Salt inside and out. For stuffing, soak rolls in milk (do not squeeze out the milk). Grind. Cream butter or margarine with egg yolks, add soaked rolls, chopped parsley (and dill if desired); add pepper, salt and nutmeg to taste. Then gently mix with egg whites beaten into a stiff froth, adding 1 T. bread crumbs. The stuffing should be rather thick. If it is not, then add more bread crumbs. Stuff the "pocket", skewer it closed, place in a roasting pan on butter and sprinkle with water. Roast in a hot oven (390°) for 1–1 $\frac{1}{2}$ hours, basting with the meat sauce and more water as the sauce evaporates. Cut nicely browned veal brisket along the ribs. Serve with boiled potatoes, and a cucumber salad or green salad.

Ingredients:

- *2 lb. veal brisket*
- *1 T. butter*

Stuffing:

- *2 stale rolls*
- *2 eggs*
- *1/2 c. milk*
- *2 T. butter or margarine*
- *1 T. finely chopped parsley*
- *1 T. chopped dill (optional)*
- *1 T. bread crumbs*
- *ground pepper*
- *salt*
- *a pinch of grated nutmeg*

Roast veal

*R*inse the meat, pat it dry, rub with garlic
crushed with salt. If the meat is flat enough,
roll it up and tie with cotton thread.
Heat the cooking oil in a frying pan and brown
the meat on all sides, then place it in a roasting
pan, add water and butter and roast
for about 1 hour in a hot oven (390°),
adding more water as the sauce evaporates.
Slice across the grain of the meat.
(If the piece of meat is rather small it
can be placed in a pot after frying
and then stewed covered with butter
and a small quantity of water until tender.)
Serve with dumplings or boiled potatoes,
and salads.

Ingredients:

- *2 lb. boneless veal
  (shoulder or rump)*
- *2–3 T. cooking oil*
- *1 T. butter*
- *garlic clove*
- *salt*

Veal cutlets with carrots and green peas

Rinse the meat and pat it dry,
slice across the grain into four thick slices,
then pound lightly until $1/2$-inch thick, forming
nice cutlets. Salt them on both sides,
dredge separately in flour, beaten egg,
and then bread crumbs; press the crumbs
in so they stick. Fry both sides
in cooking oil until golden.
When almost fried, add butter and 1 T. water
and fry a little while on a low flame.
Place a slice of lemon on each cutlet.
Serve with boiled potatoes, peas and carrots.

Peas and carrots: Clean, peel and wash
the carrots, then dice small, cover with
a small amount of boiling, slightly salted
and sweetened water and half of the butter.
If fresh or frozen peas are used they should be
added to the carrots at that point and simmered
on a low flame. If canned peas are used,
add when the carrots are tender.
Take vegetables off the flame, sprinkle
with flour, stir and cook again.
Just before serving add the remaining
butter without cooking.

Ingredients:

Veal cutlets:
- $1 1/2$ lb. boneless veal
- 2–3 T. cooking oil
- 1 T. butter
- 1 egg
- 2 T. flour
- 4–5 T. bread crumbs
- 4 lemon slices

Vegetables:
- 1 lb. carrots
- 1/2 lb. green peas (fresh, frozen or canned)
- 1 flat T. flour
- 1 T. butter
- salt
- sugar

Roast lamb

*R*inse the meat, pat it dry and cover
with cool marinade made from 3 c. water
boiled with spices and onion slices,
and vinegar added when cooled.
Keep the meat and marinade in a covered pot
and let it stand in a cool place for 2 days.
Then take the meat out of the marinade,
pat it dry, rub with salt and garlic, sprinkle
with flour, fry in very hot cooking oil
in a frying pan, place in a roasting pan
and add more cooking oil.
Roast in a hot oven (390°) for 45–50 minutes,
sprinkling the meat with the leftover
marinade from time to time.

Ingredients:

* *2 lb. lamb (with bones)*
* *2 T. flour*
* *garlic clove*
* *salt*
* *cooking oil*

Marinade:

* *1 c. vinegar*
* *a few peppercorns*
* *a few allspice seeds*
* *2 t. salt*
* *1 medium onion*

Pot roast with beets

*R*inse the meat, pat it dry, remove the gristle, lightly pound, insert sticks of salted fatback, then salt and sprinkle with flour. Heat cooking oil in a frying pan and brown the meat on all sides, then place it in a pot, add onion slices, the remaining oil and 2–3 T. water; simmer on a low flame until the onion is transparent. Add $^1/_2$ c. water, 1 t. seasoned salt and stew for about 2 hours on a low flame until tender, adding water from time to time. When the meat is tender, add the remaining flour to the sauce and cook. Serve the pot roast cut in thin slices across the grain and topped with the sauce, and with boiled potatoes and beets.

Beets: Scrub the beets with a brush, rinse and cook in boiling water until tender or else bake in an oven. Peel and grate them thick, add salt and sugar and stir in flour mixed with a few T. water. Boil, add sour cream, lemon juice or citric acid, and sugar to taste.

Ingredients:

Pot roast:
- *1 $^1/_2$ lb. boneless beef (best is rump or chuck)*
- *3 T. cooking oil*
- *2 oz. fatback*
- *2 large onions*
- *2 T. flour*
- *1 t. seasoned salt*
- *salt*

Beets:
- *1 $^1/_2$ lb. beets*
- *1 T. flour*
- *$^1/_2$ c. sour cream*
- *salt*
- *sugar*
- *lemon juice or citric acid*

Boiled beef in horseradish sauce

*R*inse the meat, put into salted boiling water and cook on a low flame. Clean and wash soup vegetables and add them to the cooking meat. Carefully wash unpeeled onion, halve it and brown over a flame, add it to the meat when it becomes tender, along with cleaned and rinsed cabbage. Cut the meat into slices across the grain. Serve with horseradish sauce, and with the vegetables taken from the bouillon if desired.

Sauce: Finely grate peeled and rinsed horseradish, add lemon juice and sugar. Mix the flour with cooled bouillon, boil, add grated horseradish, salt and sugar to taste. Bring to a boil, take off the flame and add thick sour cream. Do not boil again.

Ingredients:

- *1 ¹/₂ lb. boneless veal (chuck or rump)*
- *¹/₂ lb. cabbage*
- *¹/₂ lb. soup vegetables (carrot, parsnip, celery root, leek)*
- *1 large onion*
- *salt*
- *a few peppercorns*

Sauce:

- *¹/₄ lb. horseradish*
- *1–1¹/₂ T. flour*
- *1 c. meat bouillon*
- *¹/₂ c. sour cream*
- *salt*
- *sugar*
- *lemon juice or citric acid*

Pork cutlets with cabbage

Rinse the pork, pat it dry, cut into equal steaks, score them a few times, gently pound, salt; dredge in flour, then in egg beaten with a fork, then in bread crumbs. Form nice oval cutlets, pat the bread crumbs in so they stick. Fry both sides in pre-heated cooking oil until light golden, then add $1/2$ T. water and simmer covered on a low flame for a while. Before serving take off the cover and cook off the water. Serve with cooked cabbage.

Cooked cabbage: Discard outer leaves, carefully wash and finely chop. Add 1 c. salted boiling water and cook covered. Uncover, simmer a few minutes on a low flame and cover again. When almost tender, add peeled and chopped apples and caraway and continue to cook on a low flame. Finely chop peeled onion, fry in cooking oil until golden, add flour and mix it with the oil and then add a few T. water. Cook this mixture, add to cooked cabbage and stir. Cook all together, add salt, sugar and citric acid (optional) to taste.

Ingredients:

Pork cutlets:
- *1 1/2 lb. boneless pork*
- *2 T. cooking oil*
- *2 T. flour*
- *1 egg*
- *4–5 T. bread crumbs*

Cooked cabbage:
- *2 lb. cabbage*
- *3–4 apples (not sweet)*
- *2 medium onions*
- *2 T. flour*
- *2 T. cooking oil*
- *1 t. caraway seeds*
- *salt*
- *sugar*
- *citric acid (optional)*

Meatballs with barley groats

*R*inse the meat and pat it dry. Soak the roll in milk, squeeze out the milk and grind the meat and the rool. Add 1 egg, garlic and finely chopped onion browned in cooking oil until transparent, add pepper and salt and mix well. Form small meatballs with moistened hands, dredge in flour and fry all sides in pre-heated cooking oil. When slightly browned, add $\frac{1}{2}$ c. water, cover and stew on a low flame for 20–25 minutes, supplementing the water when needed. Serve with barley (or buckwheat) groats and sauerkraut salad.

Groats: Clean the groats, rinse and let dry in a strainer. When completely dry, sprinkle with cooking oil, drop into 2 c. boiling salted water, stir and bring to a boil quickly in the top of a double boiler directly on the burner. Cover. When groats have absorbed the water completely, fit that pot into the bottom pot with boiling water and cook on a low flame until tender.

Ingredients:

Meatballs:
- $\frac{1}{2}$ *lb. beef*
- $\frac{1}{2}$ *lb. pork*
- *1 stale roll*
- *1 egg*
- *1 medium onion*
- $\frac{1}{2}$ *c. milk*
- *2–3 T. flour*
- *2–3 T. cooking oil*
- *ground pepper*
- *salt*
- *garlic clove (optional)*

Barley groats:
- *1 c. barley*
- *1 $\frac{1}{2}$ T. cooking oil*
- *salt*

Roll-ups in bread with buckwheat groats

Rinse the meat, pat it dry, cut across the grain into four slices, pound and sprinkle with salt and pepper. Peel the onion, slice it and brown in 1 T. cooking oil until transparent, then arrange the slices on the meat fillets and cover with slices of bacon. Roll up the meat, dredge in flour, skewer, and brown on all sides in cooking oil. Place the meat in a pan, add a few T. water and the butter, and stew on a low flame for 40–45 minutes until tender. Cut off the top of the bread, hollow it, put the roll-ups with the sauce inside, top with sour cream, cover with the top of the bread and bake in the oven at 360–390° for half an hour. Serve the meat in the bread, and buckwheat groats and pickles on the side.

Groats: Clean the buckwheat groats, sprinkle with cooking oil and drop into 2 c. salted boiling water in the top half of a double boiler directly on the burner. Stir and bring to a boil quickly, then cover. When the buckwheat groats have absorbed the water completely, fit the pot into the bottom pot with boiling water and cook on a low flame until tender.

Ingredients:

Roll-ups in bread:
- *1 1/2 lb. boneless beef*
- *1 large onion*
- *4 slices bacon*
- *2–3 T. flour*
- *3–4 T. cooking oil*
- *1 T. butter*
- *ground pepper*
- *salt*
- *1/2 c. sour cream*
- *1 loaf of wholegrain bread*

Buckwheat groats:
- *1 c. buckwheat groats*
- *1–1 1/2 T. cooking oil*
- *salt*

"*Swallow nests*"

*P*ound meat into large fillets, salt
and pepper both sides and then sprinkle
generously with parsley.
Place a piece of ham and a shelled hard-boiled
egg on each fillet. Roll up and tie with white
thread, dredge in flour and quick-fry
in pre-heated cooking oil. Transfer to a pot,
add butter and some water, and stew
covered for 30–35 minutes,
supplementing water if needed.
Before serving remove the thread.
Cut each roll-up into halves across the egg.
Serve in the sauce with boiled
or mashed potatoes.

Ingredients:

- *4 large veal fillets cut across the grain (2 lb.)*
- *4 eggs*
- *3 T. finely chopped parsley*
- *4 slices fat ham*
- *2 T. flour*
- *2–3 T. cooking oil*
- *1 T. butter*
- *salt*
- *ground pepper*

Fried chicken Polonaise with Polish cucumber salad

*R*inse chicken, then quarter, salt and dredge in flour, then beaten egg and then bread crumbs. Fry on a high flame until golden, add 2–3 T. water and cook covered on a low flame until tender. Just before serving, uncover (you may add a bit of butter) and brown until skin is crispy. Serve with new potatoes and Polish cucumber salad.

Salad: Peel cucumbers, slice very thin, add sour cream mixed with salt, sugar, and vinegar (if desired). Sprinkle with chopped dill.

Ingredients:

Chickens:

- *2 small chickens*
- *5–6 T. bread crumbs*
- *3–4 T. flour*
- *1 egg*
- *salt*
- *4–5 T. cooking oil or margarine*
- *1 t. butter (optional)*

Cucumber salad:

- *1 lb. fresh cucumber*
- *1 T. finely chopped dill*
- *salt*
- *sugar*
- *1 t. wine vinegar (optional)*
- *$\frac{1}{2}$ c. sour cream*

Turkey steaks

Cut turkey breast into steaks across the grain,
pound gently to tenderize, form oval cutlets,
salt, dredge in flour and then beaten egg.
Cut stale roll into small sticks, add to bread
crumbs. Dredge cutlets on both sides in bread
crumbs and croutons, fry in pre-heated oil
until light golden, then add butter and fry
or bake a little more on low heat.
Serve with boiled potatoes and green salad.

Ingredients:

- *1 1/2 lb. turkey breast*
- *2–3 T. flour*
- *1 egg*
- *2–3 T. bread crumbs*
- *1 stale roll (without crust)*
- *3 T. cooking oil*
- *3 T. oz. butter*
- *salt*

Duck with apples

*R*inse the duck, rub inside and out with salt, pepper and marjoram. Put parsley inside. Place duck in a roasting pan, add a little butter and roast in a hot oven (480°) until nicely browned. When almost tender, pour in half of the calvados and cover tightly with aluminum foil so the duck will absorb the calvados. Peel, core and quarter the apples, then sprinkle with pepper and fry in the remaining butter. Add half-tender apples to the duck, sprinkle with the rest of the calvados and roast a little longer. Serve with boiled or roasted potatoes.

Ingredients:

- *1 young duck*
- *2–2$\frac{1}{2}$ lb. apples (green, not sweet)*
- *$\frac{1}{2}$ c. calvados*
- *2 rounded T. butter*
- *a small bunch of parsley*
- *salt*
- *ground pepper*
- *marjoram*

Carp in grey sauce

$\mathcal{S}$cale the carp and rinse outside surface, then carefully gut it, being careful not to spill the gall. Do not rinse inside. Cut into $1^1/_2$-inch steaks and salt them. Put peeled and diced celery root and sliced onion into beer diluted with 1 pt. water, add spices and a piece of lemon peel and boil until vegetables are soft (about 20 minutes). Then put in the carp sprinkled with lemon juice, and simmer on a low flame about 15–20 minutes. Take the fish out carefully and put it on a platter (keep warm). Rub the remaining fish stock through a sieve (removing pepper and allspice), add finely crumbled honey cake, plum jam, raisins and slivered almonds. Boil the sauce, add sugar to taste. Cover carp with sauce. Serve the rest of the sauce in a gravy boat. Goes well with fine buckwheat groats (*kasza krakowska*) or with boiled potatoes.

Ingredients:

- *carp (2 lb.)*
- *lemon*
- *celery root ($^1/_4$ lb.)*
- *onion ($^1/_4$ lb.)*
- *1 pt. beer*
- *2 T. butter*
- *1 T. plum jam*
- *$^1/_4$ lb. dried honey cake (optional)*
- *$^1/_4$ lb. light raisins*
- *$^1/_4$ lb. dark raisins*
- *$^1/_4$ lb. slivered almonds*
- *5–6 peppercorns*
- *5–6 allspice seeds*
- *a pinch of ginger*
- *salt*
- *sugar*

Fried carp

*R*inse and pat dry carp steaks.
Sprinkle with salt and pepper.
Beat 1 egg on a flat dish using a fork.
Dredge the steaks in flour,
then in egg and then bread crumbs.
Pat the steaks to fix the bread crumbs.
Fry until light golden.
After frying place in a hot oven or simmer
covered on a low flame for a few minutes
to make sure that the fish is well cooked inside.
Serve with mashed potatoes and horseradish.

Prepared horseradish: Grate horseradish,
season with lemon juice and sugar,
add rich sour cream.
Sour cream may be replaced with whipped
fresh cream (horseradish prepared
in this way is very light).
Carp steaks may be fried without egg
and bread crumbs, dredged in flour only.

Ingredients:

- *2 lb. carp steaks*
- *1 egg*
- *2 T. flour*
- *5–6 T. bread crumbs*
- *3 T. cooking oil or butter*
- *salt*
- *ground pepper*

Poached trout

Clean the vegetables. Boil a bouillon
of vegetables, spices and 2 pt. water.
Strain and salt the bouillon.
Gut and rinse trout, leaving heads attached.
Arrange the trout in a fish pot and pour
in hot bouillon.
Simmer on a low flame for about 15 minutes.
Place the fish on a serving platter
and pour melted butter over them, garnish
with egg slices, parsley and lemon slices.

Ingredients:

- *4 rainbow trout (approx. $^1/_2$ lb. each)*

- *$^1/_2$ lb. vegetables (carrots, celery root, parsnips, leek)*

- *1 small onion*

- *4–5 allspice seeds*

- *1–2 bay leaves*

- *2 T. butter*

- *2 hard-boiled eggs*

- *parsley and lemon slices for decoration*

Walleye baked in sour cream

*R*inse the steaks, sprinkle with salt,
dredge in flour and quick-fry in
a frying pan until golden.
Transfer to a fire-proof platter, sprinkling
with wine and melted cooking oil (or butter).
Bake covered for about 30 minutes,
sprinkling with a little water while baking.
When almost baked, pour on sour cream.

Ingredients:

- *1 1/2 lb. walleye steaks*
- *1 rounded T. flour*
- *3 T. cooking oil or butter*
- *1/2 glass white wine*
- *1/2 c. sour cream*
- *salt*

Eel in dill sauce

$\mathcal{G}$ut, remove skin, rinse and salt the eel.
Pour 3 pt. cold water into a pot
with cleaned and rinsed soup vegetables,
halved onion, bay leaf and allspice.
Boil about half an hour.
Put the fish into the boiling bouillon
and simmer another 30–35 minutes
on a low flame. Take the eel out,
place it on a serving platter and pour hot dill
sauce on it. Serve with boiled potatoes.

Dill sauce: Strain the bouillon (approx. 1 pint).
Mix the flour with a few t. water,
combine with the fish bouillon and boil,
then add dill, sour cream and butter.

Ingredients:

- *2 lb. eel*
- *$1/_2$ lb. soup vegetables (carrot, parsnip, celery root, leek)*
- *1 onion*
- *bay leaf*
- *4–5 allspice seeds*
- *3–4 T. finely chopped dill*
- *3 T. flour*
- *$1/_2$ c. sour cream*
- *1 t. butter*
- *salt*

Cabbage rolls (gołąbki) with tomato sauce

*B*oil rice until not quite tender, strain and add onion browned in cooking oil and ground pork. Add salt and pepper to taste. Place the entire cabbage (after removing the core) into a large quantity of boiling water. Carefully separate each leaf and put once again into the boiling water, a few at a time. Cook briefly, then remove with a slotted spoon and let drain. When cooled, cut out the thick part of the main vein, center the rice-and-meat filling on the leaves, fold the edges in and roll tight. Arrange *gołąbki* on cooked cabbage leaves placed on the bottom of the pot (in 2–3 layers), cover with the remaining leaves, add a cup of boiling salted water, and cook on a low flame for about 45 minutes, or else stew in the oven in a casserole, also on low heat (about 250°). When tender, discard the leaves from the top. Serve with hot tomato sauce.

Sauce: Brown finely minced onion in butter until transparent, add flour, mix, add in cold bouillon and then tomato paste. Cook on a low flame. Add salt and sugar to taste.

Ingredients:

Cabbage rolls (gołąbki):

- *1 cabbage (not very compact, approx. 3 lb.)*
- *$^1/_2$ lb. ground pork*
- *1 c. rice*
- *1 onion*
- *3 T. cooking oil*
- *salt*
- *ground pepper*

Tomato sauce:

- *2 T. tomato paste*
- *2 T. flour*
- *1 T. butter*
- *$^1/_2$ c. sour cream*
- *1 small onion*
- *1 c. bouillon*
- *salt*
- *pepper*
- *sugar*

Egg croquettes

*B*oil eggs hard (8–10 minutes),
cover with cold water.
Halve with a sharp knife, remove eggs
from the shells, being careful not to crush
the shells. Chop the eggs, add parsley
and finely chopped onion or chives, season
with salt and pepper and mix. Fill the eggshells
with egg mix, lightly pressing
with a spoon. When all shells are filled
and there is no egg mix left,
turn out the shells on a plate sprinkled
with bread crumbs so that the molds stick
to the bread crumbs flat side down.
Fry in cooking oil for a few minutes
on a medium flame, preferably covered.
Serve with fried potatoes and green salad.

Ingredients:

- *8 eggs*
- *1 medium onion
  or a bunch of chives*
- *2 T. finely chopped
  parsley*
- *2–3 T. bread crumbs*
- *salt*
- *ground pepper*
- *4 T. cooking oil*

"Vegetable bouquet"

*P*lace the cauliflower in salted, slightly sweetened boiling water, and cook until tender. Place cleaned asparagus shoots standing up in a high narrow pot, add salted, slightly sweetened boiling water, so that the tops stick out of the water. Cover and cook for 15–20 minutes.
Clean carrots, cut into sticks, cook in salted, slightly sweetened water and 1 t. butter until tender.
Cook the peas in a small quantity of salted boiling water until tender, then sprinkle with flour, cook a little longer and add 1 t. butter. Just before the vegetables are done, brown bread crumbs until golden on a dry frying pan and add melted butter. Arrange a "bouquet" of vegetables on each plate and pour the roux over the cauliflower and asparagus shoots.

Ingredients:

- *1 cauliflower*
- *$\frac{1}{2}$ lb. asparagus shoots*
- *$\frac{1}{2}$ lb. young carrots*
- *$\frac{1}{2}$ lb. green peas*
- *3 T. butter*
- *1 t. flour*
- *3 T. bread crumbs*
- *salt*
- *sugar*

Russian-style pierogi

*C*lean potatoes with a brush, cook, peel and grind together with farmer cheese. Finely chop onion and brown in cooking oil until golden, add to potato-and-cheese mixture, add salt and pepper, then mix completely. Sift the flour onto a breadboard, break 1 egg on it, add salt and approx. 1 cup lukewarm water. Knead the dough well, not very firm. Divide into parts. Roll out one part thin; cover the other parts with a bowl to protect from drying.

Cut 2-inch circles from the rolled-out dough sheet using a glass or cookie cutter. Spoon the filling into the middle of each circle, fold dough in half and pinch the edges together. Place the *pierogi* on a tray sprinkled with flour and cover with cheesecloth. Boil water in a wide, low kettle, add salt, and drop in the dumplings a few at a time. Cover, and when they rise to the surface, uncover and keep on a low flame a little longer. They will fall apart if cooked too long. Take out using a slotted spoon and sprinkle with onion browned in butter, or else fried diced fatback.

Ingredients:

Dough:
- *2–2$\frac{1}{2}$ c. flour*
- *1 egg*
- *salt*

Filling:
- *2 lb. potatoes*
- *$\frac{1}{2}$ lb. farmer cheese*
- *1 onion*
- *2 T. cooking oil*
- *salt*
- *ground pepper*

Topping:
- *2 T. butter or margarine*
- *1 onion or 2 oz. fatback*

Sauerkraut and mushroom pierogi

*R*inse the mushrooms, soak in cold water for a few hours and cook in the same water until tender.

Press the sour liquid out of the sauerkraut, chop it, add mushroom liquid and cook covered until tender. Cook off the excess water, add mushrooms cut into strips, add finely chopped onion fried in cooking oil until transparent, then add salt and pepper to taste. Sprinkle with flour and cook again. Prepare the dough as for Russian-style *pierogi* and proceed as in that recipe. Fry finely diced fatback for topping.

Ingredients:

Dough:
- *2–2 $\frac{1}{2}$ c. flour*
- *1 egg*
- *salt*

Filling:
- *1 lb. sauerkraut*
- *1 oz. dried mushrooms*
- *1 large onion*
- *1 T. flour*
- *2 T. cooking oil*
- *salt*
- *ground pepper*

Topping:
- *2 oz. fatback*

Blueberry or cherry pierogi

$\mathcal{D}$ry rinsed fruit in a strainer. Pit the cherries. Prepare the dough as for Russian-style *pierogi*. Place blueberries or cherries on the dough circles (without sugar), pinch the edges together and proceed as for Russian-style *pierogi*. Serve with melted butter, sprinkled with sugar. Serve sour cream in a separate bowl.

Pierogi with meat filling

$\mathcal{G}$rind the cooked meat, finely chop peeled onions and fry in cooking oil until transparent. Add onions to the meat together with parsley (optional), break 1 egg into it, mix in salt and pepper to taste. Prepare the dough as for Russian-style *pierogi* and proceed as in that recipe. Top with melted butter of fried diced fatback.

Ingredients:

Blueberry or cherry pierogi:
Dough:
- *2–2 1/2 c. flour*
- *1 egg*
- *salt*

Stuffing:
- *1 lb. blueberries or cherries*
- *2–4 T. sugar to sprinkle*

Topping:
- *1 T. melted butter*
- *1/2 c. sour cream*

Pierogi with meat filling:
Dough:
- *2–2 1/2 c. flour*
- *1 egg*
- *salt*

Filling:
- *3/4 lb. cooked meat*
- *2 T. cooking oil*
- *2 onions*
- *1 egg*
- *1 T. finely chopped parsley (optional)*
- *salt*
- *ground pepper*

Topping:
- *2 T. butter or 2 oz. fatback*

Kopytka
(potato dumplings)

*B*oil peeled potatoes in salted water, drain,
mash with milk, 1 rounded t. butter
and a pinch of salt, then leave to cool.
When cool, grind, place on a breadboard,
break 1 egg and sift some flour on it.
Knead the dough quickly, adding the remaining
flour a little at a time. Boil water in a large
wide pot, so that the *kopytka* can be dropped
immediately into hot water as soon as they
are cut, because the dough soon gets damp.
Form long fingers of dough, flatten slightly
and cut at an angle into bite-size pieces.
Put them in boiling salted water a few at a time.
When they rise to the surface, take out
with a slotted spoon and place in a large bowl,
adding some butter to each portion
so they do not stick together,
and gently shake the bowl.
Keep covered until all *kopytka* are cooked.
Serve with meat and sauce or as a separate
dish with mushroom or tomato sauce.
They are also tasty fried in cooking oil.

Ingredients:

- *$2\frac{1}{4}$ lb. potatoes*
- *$1\frac{3}{4}$ c. flour*
- *1 egg*
- *1 rounded T. butter*
- *3 T. milk*
- *salt*

Potato croquettes with mushroom sauce

*B*rush and rinse potatoes, cook whole and unpeeled, leave to cool and then peel them. Grind, add eggs, flour, and chopped onion browned in cooking oil. Add salt and pepper to taste and mix into a smooth mass. Form the mass into a thick roll on a breadboard, cut into pieces and form oval, medium-size croquettes, dredge in bread crumbs and fry both sides in hot cooking oil until golden. Serve with mushroom sauce.

Sauce: soak carefully cleaned mushrooms in cold water for a few hours. Cook in the same water, save the liquid and chop the mushrooms. Fry finely minced onion in cooking oil until transparent, mix with chopped mushrooms, sprinkle with flour, add cold mushroom liquid and cook, then mix in sour cream and add salt and pepper to taste.

Ingredients:

Potato croquettes:
- $2^1/_2$ *lb. potatoes*
- *1 T. cooking oil*
- *1 onion*
- *2 eggs*
- *5 T. flour*
- *1 T. finely chopped parsley*
- *2–3 T. bread crumbs*
- *3–4 T. cooking oil*
- *salt*
- *ground pepper*

Sauce:
- *1 oz. dried mushrooms*
- *1 small onion*
- *3 T. cooking oil*
- *3 T. flour*
- *$1/_2$ c. sour cream*
- *salt*
- *ground pepper*

Potato pancakes

$\mathcal{P}$eel and rinse potatoes, finely grate,
then lightly press out some of the water.
Add grated onion, 1 egg, flour, salt and pepper
and mix. Heat cooking oil or lard
in a frying pan until very hot, fry flattened
dollops of potato mixture quickly on both sides.
Best if served right from the frying pan,
with sour cream.
May be served with coleslaw
or mushroom sauce.
If you wish to serve the pancakes with sugar
or jam, omit onion and pepper.

Ingredients:

- *3 lb. potatoes*
- *1 onion*
- *1 egg*
- *2 T. flour*
- *salt*
- *ground pepper*
- *cooking oil for frying*

Pierogi leniwe ("lazy pierogi")

Grind farmer cheese into a bowl, then add egg yolks and salt. Beat egg whites into a stiff froth and stir in alternately with the cheese and sifted flour, then mix. Turn out the pastry on a breadboard, form 1-inch-thick rolls, slightly flatten, cross-hatch with the dull side of a knife, then cut at an angle into bite-size pieces and drop into boiling, salted water. When they rise to the surface, take out with a slotted spoon. Serve with melted butter with browned bread crumbs.

Ingredients:

- *1 1/2 lb. farmer cheese*
- *2–3 eggs*
- *1 1/2 c. flour*
- *salt*
- *1 T. bread crumbs*
- *1 T. butter*

Sauerkraut and mushroom crepes

*B*reak the eggs into sifted flour, add cooking oil and salt, pour in milk and mix in a blender until the batter is smooth. Add water gradually, depending on how thick the batter is. Cover the batter with a towel and leave for 30–60 minutes. Then fry crepes on a non-stick frying pan (or a regular frying pan greased with a piece of fatback). Crepes should spread over the entire surface of the frying pan. Fill the ready crepes and roll them up, then dredge the rolled crepes in beaten egg and then bread crumbs. Just before serving, quick-fry both sides in hot cooking oil.

Filling: Rinse dried mushrooms, soak in a small quantity of cold water for a few hours and cook in the same water until tender. Save the liquid. Press sour liquid out of the sauerkraut, add mushroom stock and cook covered on low heat. When tender, cook off excess liquid, add mushrooms cut into thin strips, finely chopped onion (first browned in cooking oil until transparent), and add salt and pepper to taste. Sprinkle with flour and cook a little longer.

Ingredients:

Batter:
- *2 eggs*
- *1 ½ c. flour*
- *1 T. cooking oil*
- *1 c. milk*
- *½ c. water*
- *salt*
- *a piece of fatback to grease frying pan (optional)*

Filling:
- *1 lb. sauerkraut*
- *2 oz. dried mushrooms*
- *1 large onion*
- *1 T. flour*
- *2 T. cooking oil*
- *salt*
- *ground pepper*

For frying ready crepes:
- *1 egg*
- *bread crumbs*
- *cooking oil*

Cheese crepes

*G*rind the cheese, add powdered sugar,
vanilla sugar and egg yolks, and mix
into a smooth mass, then add raisins
and orange peel.
Spread the mixture on the crepes,
roll up or fold into triangles.
Serve after frying lightly.
Sprinkle with powdered sugar.
Top with sour cream if desired.
Many people like them best
with cherry preserves.

Ingredients:

Batter:

- *as for sauerkraut
  and mushroom crepes*

Filling:

- *1 lb. farmer cheese*

- *2 egg yolks*

- *3 T. sugar*

- *2–3 T. raisins*

- *1 T. finely chopped
  candied orange peel*

- *vanilla sugar*

- *powdered sugar
  to sprinkle*

- *sour cream (optional)*

Apple fritters (racuszki)

*A*dd egg yolks, a pinch of salt and
1 T. olive oil to sifted flour. Pour milk in,
still mixing. Mix the batter in a blender
and leave for 15 minutes covered with a towel.
Peel and core apples and cut into $1/4$-inch slices.
Whisk egg whites into a stiff froth,
gently mix with the batter, which should be
smooth like thick cream.
Dip apple slices in the dough, put in hot
cooking oil and fry on a moderate flame
until light golden on both sides.
Sprinkle with vanilla sugar and powdered sugar
immediately after removing
from the frying pan. Serve hot.

Ingredients:

- *1 lb. apples (not sweet)*
- *1 c. flour*
- *2 eggs*
- *1 T. olive oil*
- *$3/4$ c. milk*
- *salt*
- *cooking oil*
- *powdered sugar
  and vanilla sugar
  to sprinkle*

Plum-filled potato dumplings (knedle)

$\mathcal{R}$inse plums and remove pits. Dry the plums in a strainer. Peel, boil and drain potatoes, add 1 t. butter and grind or mash. Break the egg into the potato mass when cooled, add salt, sifted flour and potato starch, quickly knead dough smooth. Form a thick dough roll and cut piece by piece. Pat each piece flat in flour-dusted hands. Roll a plum in each piece and place it on a floured board. Put a few at a time into boiling salted water. When they rise to the surface they are ready. Remove using a slotted spoon. Serve with melted butter or topped with sour cream and sprinkle with powdered sugar.

Ingredients:

- *2 lb. potatoes*
- *$1\frac{1}{2}$ c. flour*
- *1 T. potato starch*
- *1 egg*
- *1 T. butter*
- *salt*
- *$1\frac{1}{2}$ lb. plums*
- *sugar to sprinkle*
- *sour cream to top (optional)*

Yeast-raised babka

*M*ix the yeast with 1 t. sugar and a few T. warm milk, cover with a towel and leave in a warm place to grow.
Add salt to dry sifted flower, pour in the yeast and the rest of the lukewarm milk, gently mix and leave for a few minutes.
When it has risen, add egg yolks mixed with sugar and grated lemon peel and mix in a blender until smooth (about 10 minutes).
Still mixing, gradually add melted, still-warm butter, then add orange peel and raisins.
When the dough has completely absorbed the butter, cover it with a towel and leave in a warm place for about 1 hour.
When it doubles in volume, put it in a tall hollow-centered cake form, greased with butter and sprinkled with bread crumbs.
The form should be filled a bit less than half of its height. Cover the pan with a towel.
When the dough has almost filled the form, brush the top with an egg mixed with 1 t. milk and put into a moderate oven.
Bake for about 40–45 minutes at 360°.
When cooled, remove from the form and glaze.

Glaze: Mix powdered sugar with lemon juice and hot water.
Note: The above amount is enough to make 2 *babkas*: 1 large (about 10 inches in diameter) and 1 small (about 7 inches in diameter).

Ingredients:

Dough:

- *1 lb. wheat flour*
- *1 c. sugar*
- *³/₄ c. butter or margarine*
- *5 egg yolks*
- *1 c. milk*
- *2 oz. yeast*
- *¹/₂ flat t. salt*
- *2 oz. raisins*
- *1 T. finely chopped candied orange peel, grated lemon peel (scalded with hot water)*
- *1 egg to brush the* babka
- *butter and bread crumbs to grease the cake form*

Glaze:

- *1 c. powdered sugar*
- *1 T. lemon juice*
- *1 T. boiling water*

Poppy seed roll

*R*inse poppy seeds, scald with hot water
and let sit overnight. The next day,
prepare dough as for yeast-raised *babka*
but a little more firm and let it rise.
Drain the poppy seeds in a sieve,
grind at least three times.
Melt butter in a pot, add sugar, poppy seeds,
honey, raisins, nuts and candied orange peel
and fry a few minutes on a low flame,
still mixing.
When slightly cooled, add egg whites whisked
into a froth and mix. Divide the dough
and the poppy seed mixture into three parts.
Roll out each part of the dough,
lightly sprinkled with flour.
Evenly spread poppy seed mixture
on the dough, roll up the dough and place
in long, approx. 18-inch loaf pans. The edges
should be tucked under the dough roll.
Let the rolls rise in a warm place covered
with a towel, then brush with an egg
mixed with 1 t. milk.
Bake in a moderate oven (360°)
for 35–40 minutes. Check if ready
with a toothpick, which should remain dry.
When slightly cooled, take out of
the pans and glaze.

Ingredients:

Dough:
- *1 lb. flour*
- *1 c. sugar*
- *³/₄ c. margarine*
- *3 egg yolks*
- *1 c. milk*
- *1 oz. yeast*
- *grated lemon peel (scalded with water)*
- *salt*
- *butter and bread crumbs to coat the forms*

Filling:
- *1 lb. poppy seeds*
- *1 c. sugar*
- *2 T. honey*
- *1 rounded T. butter*
- *2 egg whites*
- *vanilla sugar*
- *³/₄ c. raisins*
- *1 c. chopped walnuts*
- *1 T. finely chopped candied orange peel*

Brushing:
- *1 egg*

Glaze:
- *1 c. powdered sugar*
- *1 T. lemon juice*
- *1–2 T. boiling water*

Honey-spice cake

Cream butter in a large bowl, add egg yolks, sugar and spices and mix until smooth. Pour in liquid honey, coffee and lemon juice and continue to mix for a while, then mix soda with sifted flour. Add figs, orange peel, walnuts and raisins to the egg-and-butter mixture and mix all together. Beat egg whites into a froth and spoon alternately with spoonfuls of flour into the mixture, still stirring. Pour the dough into two loaf pans (10 inches x 5 inches) greased with butter and sprinkled with bread crumbs, and place them immediately in a pre-heated (300°) oven. When the dough has risen, increase the temperature bake in a moderate oven (360°). Do not disturb while baking for about 40 minutes. Before taking out, check with a toothpic. The toothpick should remain dry. When slightly cooled, take out of the loaf pan. Honey-spice cake will last as long as 2–3 weeks tightly wrapped in aluminum foil.

Ingredients:

- *1 lb. flour*
- *4 eggs*
- *1 c. honey*
- *1 c. sugar*
- *$\frac{1}{2}$ c. butter or margarine*
- *2 t. instant coffee*
- *juice of $\frac{1}{2}$ lemon*
- *1 t. baking soda*
- *2 t. spices consisting of cloves, cinnamon, cardamom, pepper and nutmeg*
- *2 T. chopped walnuts*
- *2 T. finely chopped candied orange peel*
- *2 T. figs cut into thin strips*
- *2 T. raisins*
- *butter and bread crumbs to grease the loaf pan*

Fruit cake

*M*ix butter and eggs with sugar
and vanilla sugar in a bowl.
Add raisins, walnuts, orange peel and figs,
slightly sprinkled with flour.
Line a loaf pan with parchment paper greased
with butter or margarine. Whisk egg whites
into a stiff froth, add flour/baking powder
and egg whites alternately to the bowl
a spoon at a time, gently stirring.
Place the mixture in the loaf pan and bake
in a moderate oven (360°–390°) for about
35–45 minutes. Check with a toothpick.
If the toothpick is dry, the cake is ready.
After slightly cooling and taking out of the pan,
glaze and sprinkle with slivered almonds.

Ingredients:

Dough:

- *$\frac{1}{2}$ lb. sifted flour*
- *1 c. sugar*
- *4 eggs*
- *$\frac{1}{2}$ c. butter or margarine*
- *2 flat t. baking powder*
- *$\frac{1}{4}$ c. raisins*
- *$\frac{1}{4}$ c. chopped walnuts*
- *$\frac{1}{4}$ c. candied orange peel*
- *3–4 figs cut into thin strips*
- *vanilla sugar*
- *a few slivered almonds for decoration*
- *parchment paper to line the pan*

Glaze:

- *$\frac{1}{2}$ c. powdered sugar*
- *1 T. hot water*

Cheese cake

*Q*uickly knead dough from the listed ingredients, roll in aluminum foil and leave in the fridge for half an hour. Cream butter with sugar in a large bowl, adding egg yolks, one at a time, still mixing. Grind the cheese, add to butter-and-egg mixture, then add vanilla extract and mix until smooth. Add candied orange peel and rinsed raisins.

Take out the dough from the fridge and halve it. Roll out one half to fill the bottom of the cake pan, pierce with a fork here and there and bake at 360° for about 25 minutes until light golden. Form pencil-thin strips from the rest of the dough.

Whisk egg whites into a stiff froth and gently mix with the cheese mixture, then place on the baked crust and arrange the dough strips on top, forming a checkered pattern. Brush with lightly beaten egg white. Place in a pre-heated medium oven (about 360°) and bake for 50 minutes. When ready, open the oven and leave it open for a few minutes, then take out the cheese cake. Remove from the pan when cooled.

Ingredients:

Dough:
- $\frac{1}{2}$ *lb. flour*
- $\frac{1}{2}$ *c. margarine*
- $\frac{1}{2}$ *c. powdered sugar*
- *2 egg yolks*
- *1 grated lemon peel*

Cheese mixture:
- *1 $\frac{3}{4}$ lb. farmer cheese*
- $\frac{1}{2}$ *c. butter*
- *5 eggs*
- *1 $\frac{1}{4}$ c. sugar*
- *vanilla extract*
- $\frac{1}{2}$ *c. raisins*
- *2–3 T. finely chopped candied orange peel*

Brushing:
- *1 egg white*

Faworki or chrust

$\mathcal{A}$dd egg yolks, 1 egg, baking soda, liquor, salt and sour cream to the flour sifted on a breadboard. Knead the dough smooth. Separate $^1/_4$ of the dough, cover the rest with a bowl. Roll out the dough very thin, as this is essential for the quality of the *faworki*. The dough should be as thin as parchment. Cut the dough into 1-inch strips with a sharp knife, then cut the strips at an angle into 4- or 5-inch pieces. Make an inch-long slot in the middle of each piece and twist one end through the hole. Proceed with the other quarters of the dough in the same way. Arrange the ready *faworki* on a floured baking sheet or breadboard and cover with a clean dishtowel.

Melt lard in a wide low pot. Begin to fry when the lard is well heated, which can be checked by dropping a piece of rolled out dough into it. It should expand rapidly and get light yellow.

Drop in the *faworki* a few at a time, turn with a wooden skewer and take out when light golden. Place them on a layer of paper towels to get rid of excess grease, then generously sprinkle with powdered sugar and vanilla sugar.

Ingredients:

Dough:
- *2$^1/_2$ lb. flour*
- *3 egg yolks*
- *1 egg*
- *$^1/_2$ t. baking soda*
- *$^1/_2$ c. sour cream*
- *1 shot glass rum or vodka*
- *a pinch of salt*
- *1$^3/_4$ lb. lard for frying*
- *powdered sugar and vanilla sugar to sprinkle*

Ex libris

Galeria Polskiej Książki Sp. z o. o.

ul. Dęblińska 13
04-187 Warszawa
ph. (22) 610-85-95, fax (22) 612-02-86
e-mail: exlibris@exlibris-pl.com
www.exlibris-pl.com

Recipes by
ALINA FEDAK

Translation by
MAŁGORZATA WALCZAK, MICHAEL JACOBS, Letterman

Photographs
G-M STUDIO
MAREK GERSTMANN, JERZY MALINOWSKI

The pictured courses were prepared by the Flik Restaurant.
Chef
MIROSŁAW RESZCZYK

Food presentation by
ROMANA DANIEL

Editing
PaArt
Design
look STUDIO

© Ex Libris Galeria Polskiej Książki Sp. z o.o.
Warszawa 2007
ISBN 978-83-88455-44-5

The photographers wish to thank
Rosenthal Wedgwood
Zepter Poland
Dom Handlowy „Banasik"
for graciously providing tableware.